Lend a Hand

by Mary Lindeen

Table of Contents

At Home 2

At School 4

In the Community 6

On the Planet 12

Glossary 16

Consultant:
Adria F. Klein, Ph.D.
California State University, San Bernardino

capstone classroom

Heinemann Raintree • Red Brick Learning
division of Capstone

At Home

People help each other in many ways. Members of a family know how to help each other. This girl is washing dishes.

This family just moved. They are working together to carry boxes. They will make this new house feel like home.

At School

Teachers are good helpers. This teacher is helping his students become better readers. This student is helping by listening and doing her best work.

This teacher is helping adults learn to speak English. She is a **volunteer**. She enjoys spending her time helping others.

In the Community

This boy has some clothes that do not fit him anymore. He is sorting them to give away to another family in need.

Some people give money to **charity**. Other people help deliver meals to people who are hungry. **Community** members help each other.

Every community has many helpers who live and work there. This is a dentist. She helps people keep their teeth clean and healthy.

People in this community are helping to build a new house for a family who needs it.

This person is working in a community garden. The whole **neighborhood** helps plant and take care of the garden. They all enjoy the garden at harvest time.

These children are having a toy drive. They are working together to **raise** money and gather toys to help other children in need.

On the Planet

No matter who you are or where you live, you can do things to help take care of our planet. Planting a garden in your yard helps clean the air and protect the soil.

Taking time to **recycle** glass, plastic, cardboard and other materials also helps the planet.

These boys are working together to clean up a park. This keeps the land clean for people and animals. It is a great way to help the planet.

When everyone lends a hand and works together, our world is a better place. It is a safer, more beautiful, more fun place to live!

Glossary

charity	a group that raises money to help people in need
community	a group of people who live in the same area
neighborhood	the area or section in a community where people live
raise	to collect money for a charity or other group
recycle	to sort old items so that they can be made into new items
volunteer	to offer to do a job without pay